The Butterfly Is Me!

A Collection of Inspirational Poems

Written By Margaret Ann Stanton
Cancer Patient

Bloomington, IN Milton Keynes, UK

AuthorHouse™
1663 Liberty Drive, Suite 200
Bloomington, IN 47403
www.authorhouse.com
Phone: 1-800-839-8640

AuthorHouse™ UK Ltd.
500 Avebury Boulevard
Central Milton Keynes, MK9 2BE
www.authorhouse.co.uk
Phone: 08001974150

© *2006 Margaret Ann Stanton. All rights reserved.*

No part of this book may be reproduced, stored in a retrieval system, or transmitted by any means without the written permission of the author.

First published by AuthorHouse 12/14/2006

ISBN: 978-1-4259-4595-4 (sc)

Printed in the United States of America
Bloomington, Indiana

This book is printed on acid-free paper.

Cover Photo Taken By: Gregory M. Cohen

This book is dedicated to all those who have suffered from Inflammatory Breast Cancer and to their family members, and to all of the people who helped with Peg's Journey, both medically and spiritually, and also to her loving family, friends and students.

Please take some time to visit the Inflammatory Breast Cancer Memorial Site located at: www.ibcmemorial.org. This website has both pictures and personal stories of those who have become pathfinders from Inflammatory Breast Cancer.

About the Author:
Margaret Stanton

Peg was an excellent teacher who taught both in & out of the classroom. She taught for 35 years in the Central Bucks School District in Pennsylvania where she helped to develop a new program for gifted students in grades 1-6. Outside of the classroom she taught many people, children and adults, the value of friendship, strength, and courage. Peg's life was a series of lessons to her beloved children, to her devoted husband, to her numerous friends and family and to herself. Her classroom was never confined to 4 walls as she taught many to "think outside of the box". She made such a positive impact on others that the week before she passed approximately 200 people, including family, friends, other teachers, prior students and their parents visited her house to say their goodbyes. There was a special Christmas where her students knew she would not be able to decorate her house for the holidays because of rigorous chemotherapy. When Peg was out getting chemotherapy, her students decorated her house from top to bottom with many Christmas lights. They also filled her living room with poinsettias and her refrigerator with food. After she returned home, they all gathered on her front porch and sang carols to her, complete with one student who accompanied them on the trumpet. This was truly a Christmas Miracle! These are just some examples of how people responded to her, since she gave so much to them.

In 1999, Peg was diagnosed with an extremely rare form of breast cancer, a monster named "inflammatory breast cancer". Only about 1% to 6%[1] of breast cancers are inflammatory breast cancer (ibc). Her treatments included a radical mastectomy, chemotherapy, radiation and a grueling bone marrow stem cell transplant. Peg tried chemo after chemo, but to no avail, the monster kept spreading. She faced head on each treatment option and never questioned why she was chosen to suffer. Instead she began a journey to help her find an inner peace. Peg traveled with her daughter Kristina to Lourdes, France and with her husband Joe to Hawaii, Alaska, England and throughout the Midwestern United States, especially Sedona, Arizona and several Native American reservations.

It was in Sedona, where a butterfly landed on her shoulder and became her "symbol". A butterfly, for its size is one of the strongest animals, yet is still delicate and graceful. Butterflies migrate thousands of miles each year and most importantly, they are free. Peg found many correlations between herself and the butterfly, hence the title, "The Butterfly Is Me".

Peg lost her battle with the dreadful disease and became a pathfinder on Sunday January 23, 2005.

It was during her six year journey with cancer that Peg started to write the poems found in this book. They are reflections about her and about life. She hoped that other cancer patients or anyone struggling with life would find these poems helpful and inspiring.

Please enjoy them!

Pictures of Peg and her Friends and Family

Stanton Family Photo by the Pool in Doylestown, PA
Left to Right: Front Row: Charlie
Middle Row: Peg, Helen, Clement
Back Row: Robert, Patty, James

Easter Sunday 1947
Left to Right: Helen Stanton
(Peg's Mom), Peg, and Patty (Peg's Sister)

Peg and Her 2 Kids Singing by the Piano
Michael, Kristie, Peg

4 Generations in Valdosta, GA Aug 1972

Left to Right: Peg, Kristie, Ethel, Helen
Ethel (Peg's Grandmother)
Kristie (Peg's Daughter)
(Ethel, Helen and Kristie were all born on March 24)

Peg, Kristie and Michael 1980s
Photo Taken by Henry Wein

Joe Harosky and Peg
in Sitka, Alaska

Peg and Kristie
in Paris, France 2003

Peg and Kristie, Easter 2003

**Kristie, Peg and Fran Szabo
(Peg's Best Friend since High School)**

2004 Susan G. Komen Race for the Cure in Philadelphia, PA

Michael, Peg, Kristie
August 2004 at Peg's 60th Birthday Party

Contents

A Walk in the Woods	14
The Garden of Life	17
My Journey with Cancer	20
The Jigsaw	25
Hot Air Balloon	27
The Butterfly Is Me	30
Miracles Abound	32
Love on a Mountain Top	34
Facts About Inflammatory Breast Cancer	37
Disclaimer	43

A Walk in the Woods
Written November 11, 2002

As I wander through the woods on a path to the golden light
I am aware of the beauty of nature that surrounds me.
The sounds of the gentle wind and the birds in flight
Excite the spirit that is within me.

I smell the dampness of the soil beneath my feet
And I am drawn toward the waterfall ahead.
The leaves in their full majestic splendor are there to meet
This soul with their array of colors, gold and red.

As I approach the stream with its gentle rush of water
I see my guides waiting there to lead me
To show me the universe with every son and daughter
Floating in the glory and of souls that are free.

The butterfly alights on my shoulder
To give me courage to move along
Its presence makes me feel a little bolder
And my heart is filled with song.

The song is of life and beauty and strength
Of courage and wonder and universal love
As I sing the song along the path's illuminated length
I am filled with the wonder of all that is above.

The guides are surrounded in the light of God
And wave me onward to the water's sound
Where I see my loved ones with smiles that are broad
And they greet me with joy and peace all around.

There in the glistening waterfall
I see the light beckoning me near
I listen with joy to the sound of the call
And I approach without any fear.

I feel light and am lifted up on high
To the top of the world above the tree
Up to the clear and beautiful sky
And I feel myself soaring. I am free.

I look around at the world so clear
And see my life as it is right now
And all of those that I hold dear
I honor them with a reverent bow.

They all have been there through this journey of life
Teaching me love and patience and the spirit of giving
They have helped me through good times and those of strife
They have taught me what it means to be living.

I will not leave them when I move on
They are my heart and will always be there
We are connected with a very strong bond
And they will feel me whispering in the air.

The gentle breeze that touches their face
Will be my spirit telling them I am near
To love them and thank them for their beautiful grace
I will be waiting to greet them with the love that is here.

As I float along in this holy space
I know that angels and guides will be there for me
But my work is not done in the worldly place
And I will return to the earth with its mountains and sea

The light of God gently lowers me down
To the sights and sounds of the life below
And as my feet softly touch the ground
I feel the love of the spirit in the warm, radiant glow.

As the waterfall and loved ones begin to fade
My butterfly alights on my shoulder again
And leads me back to them through a glorious glade
To continue my life through the sunshine and rain

I embrace the world with a new found energy
And I set about to learn to connect
To appreciate all and work for the synergy
Of mankind and God who I will not neglect.

It is time to embrace the world and those who are here
To give and receive with kindness and love
To know that divine acceptance is abundantly clear
When we are in touch with the One up above

I continue this journey with joy in my heart
And try to forgive and to find peace within
To understand what I need to start
I give you my love and peace and joy. Amen

The Garden of Life
Written November, 2002

As I walk through the garden of life,
I am enrapt by the contrasts and the beauty therein.
Along the way there are weeds and thorns
But the flowers are wonderful in their colorful skin.

The sun shines down to warm my soul,
While the gentle wind caresses my face.
The sounds of the birds singing their song
Brings joy and peace to this wonderful place.

A butterfly flits by to alight on a shrub,
And it unfolds its colorful wings.
It signals a delicacy and enormous strength
To a soul on a journey to marvelous things.

The path through the garden is not always easy
For the weeds and the thorns reach out to touch
To bring pain and sorrow to those who come near
And the soul cries out 'cause the burden's so much.

But as I move through and pick up the debris
I slowly remove the obstacles that are there
The work is slow and the thorns can prick
And at times the dark clouds fill the air.

The chore is hard and my back is bent
And I wonder why I care to clear the space
The weeds will grow back, but somehow I know
That I can create for myself a beautiful place.

A place where I can find joy and peace
As I look around at the miracle of life
And the work is worth all of the energy and time
Because the love in my heart drowns out the strife.

And as the weeds return to crowd out the beauty
It is easier for me to pull up their stalks
I am freer now to enjoy nature's gifts
And to savor All in my many walks.

I am learning that to be part of the beauty
My spirit needs to be cleared of its weeds
By thinking and praying and thanking the Divine
I become aware of what it is on which my soul feeds.

Though the work is never totally finished
I try not to worry about the future or past
Today is the present and I will focus myself
On the colors and sounds that will forever last.

On the days when I feel my spirit sink
I will walk in the garden of eternal love
I will see that God is helping me
To move my soul to the skies above.

To breathe in the warm scented fragrances
And to watch the rose unfold
To see the dew nourish the flower
Is to see my soul grow bold.

Though I am not afraid of what is beyond
I am not ready to leave and abandon my tasks
My chapel is the garden with all that is there
It is a place where I can learn to remove the masks.

I want to discover the me that is real
To live in this life and find my soul
It is then that time and space will dissolve
And I will find my spirit, healing and whole.

It is with joy that I approach the dawn of each day
My problems will be ever diminished
My strength of spirit will get me through
Until my work is finished.

If I could give you a wonderful gift
It would be to look inside
And to see the wonderful person who is there
In the body where your spirit and soul reside.

Look to the garden as I have done
Pull out the weeds and enjoy the scene
It is then that you will understand
What this journey of life will truly mean.

Enjoy the flowers and birds and trees
And know that you have a power within
To know yourself and heal the wounds
And to let a spiritual quest begin.

God is with us in energy and strength
We must open ourselves up to feel His power
And when we appreciate what we can do
Our hearts will blossom just like the flower

So together we move through the garden of life
Each choosing the flower that heals and protects
Discovering the beauty and songs that are there
Moving ever closer to God whom we must never neglect

This journey is all about who we are
And what role we must play
We are the gardeners of our souls
Live with joy and enlightenment today.

My Journey with Cancer
Written December, 2002

Oh, how life changed while I was sleeping
The days were planned and there was work ahead
There was laughter and joy; there was no weeping.
Then the word CANCER reared its ugly head.

I heard the words, and shouted Oh God, why me?
Anger, disbelief, denial and fears
How could I have cancer? It is not meant to be.
There is too much to do to shed any tears.

I, who rarely had problems with my health,
I, who was not sick since I was a child,
This cancer crept up with a quiet stealth
I was calm on the outside, but inside I went wild.

What did I do that would get this disease?
Could I have changed it if I knew it was coming?
The mammograms and tests were done with ease
And how my heart is wildly drumming.

I, who had many things to complete,
I, who had a new life just taking hold,
I will fight and not face a cancerous defeat
I will do all that I can with steps that are bold.

I moved through my life drowning out that word
With a flurry of treatments designed to heal
But "Inflammatory breast cancer" is what I heard
They are not talking about me; this cannot be real.

My bouts with chemotherapy were quickly begun
I weathered the treatments, but lost my hair
Wasn't that enough to convince me this would be a long run?
But I kept up my courage; I did not despair.

The wave of emotions moved like a tide
Courage and bravery, turmoil and fear
I felt as though I was on a roller coaster ride
But denial kept me from shedding a tear.

I soon found myself under the surgeon's knife
I lost twenty lymph nodes and most of my breast
But still believed cancer would not steal my life
I was strong and would be able to withstand the test.

More chemo was called for
and fatigue began to set in
But I knew I was able to fight this war
I believed that I would eventually win.

Radiation came next with it killing rays
To burn out the cancer and make me well
I could face this as just the next phase
Of a journey that has taken me to the edge of hell.

I did all that was asked and they wanted more
A bone marrow transplant would secure my fate
I wanted the cancer gone; I wanted a cure
I prayed that these attempts were not too late.

For three weeks in the hospital the chemo dripped in
So sick that I wondered why I was doing all of this
But maybe I wasn't ready to give in
There was so much of life I wasn't ready to miss.

I came home to recover and to build up my strength
Thinking that the battle was **finally** won.
I looked back at the year; a **time of** great length
But I did it all and was getti**ng ready** to run.

Then within a month inflammation appeared
On my arms and the wall of my chest
Inflammatory breast cancer is more than I feared
Can I go on and do for me what is best?

Throughout this ordeal I continued to teach
But the fatigue was wearing me down
The end of the day I could barely reach
I tried to be cheerful, tried not to frown.

More chemotherapy in the form of a pill
And chemical burns appeared on my hands and feet
I could barely walk; this journey up hill
Even then the denial allowed me to be upbeat.

I lost the nails on my toes and fingers
But vanity was never a part of me
I could beat this disease; it did not have to linger
Soon I would be cancer free.

The inflammation began to subside
And hope was ever more strong
I knew I could last on this terrible ride
It would be over before much too long.

But for a year and a half it kept on returning
And different treatments were in store
The whole time I felt myself yearning
To be rid of this cancer; I wanted no more.

I finally decided I had to retire
I could not keep up the pace
I never was very much of a crier,
But I was finally losing the race.

I look back at the support that was there for me
To people who have blessed me with their care
I realize love is a therapy
A gift that is ever so rare.

Denial is gone; my time running out
But I have found joy in so many places
I want to run and scream and shout;
And smile at all of the loving faces.

A spiritual quest has taken over for me
And I find an energy that is heaven sent
I can face myself and be set free
And know that my life has been well spent.

I can face the world without being scared
I have run the gamut of emotion
My courage is real now because I have dared
To rise above earthly commotion.

I am finding joy and peace and love
That comes from a Universal One
I am not afraid of looking above
And I know my life is not done.

I may be getting to leave this earthly plane
But my soul will never die
I will live forever in sunshine and rain
And will be part of the rainbow in the sky.

My life continues and I shall live
As part of a universal spirit
I have learned to love and to forgive
And my life will have no limit.

I have feared the trials that this life had in store
I will be ready to move to a higher place
I am willing to fight the battle some more
But I will move on with love and a new – found grace.

Cancer has been a two edged sword
I have been frightened but also I am strong
I have found a light and can move on toward
A world of spirit with a joyful song.

The Jigsaw
Written December, 2002

Life is a jigsaw puzzle that challenges me along the way
At times the pieces fall into place and are easy to see
But at other times the jumble of confusion keeps me away
From finding out where all of the pieces must be.

I attack the enigma with a sense of completing the task
Only to discover that I grow weary and want to stop
Not knowing where to look, or who to ask
Sometimes I just throw up the pieces and watch them drop.

To add to the problem, the pieces are bare
Until I place them where they belong.
Then they take on the colors of nature so fair
And finding my way is ever more strong.

I do not know when I begin
What scene will develop when all is through
Mistakes and patience will help me win
And I'll be able to see how much I grew.

As the picture emerges I see my life unfold
There is chaos and beauty, turmoil and strength
A picture of me is being told
As I find the pieces along the width and length.

I see the pain and feel the sorrow
And clouds in the picture appear
To blot out any sense of tomorrow
Which only accelerates my fear.

I see my mistakes and what could have been done
And how many choices I thoughtlessly made
So many opportunities for good are gone
And my times to correct them are beginning to fade.

But as I create the world that is mine
I know that life is a series of lessons
I have learned and grown in a way that is fine
And felt the warmth of God's many blessings.

The puzzle is almost completed
And I love what I see
I did not allow myself to be defeated
And I am who I am supposed to be.

The beauty and peace in the picture are me
I worked hard to get the pieces in place
And now my spirit is setting me free
To be part of the universe, without time and space.
My angel's wings are wrapped around
And gently hold me tight,
There is a new wisdom I have found
And everything will be all right.

My picture takes on a warm and comforting glow
And doves of peace are surrounding me
I feel that I am getting ready to go
To discover more of what I will be.

I am part of the rainbows, the flowers and sky
I am part of the spirit from the Power above
And my soul is ever lifting on high
The puzzle is done…The picture is Love.

Hot Air Balloon
Written December, 2002

I approach the waiting hot air balloon
Weighed down by my doubts and fear
The beautiful colors present themselves
As if a rainbow did appear.

As I step inside I feel my self gently lifting up
And watch the world take on a different view
I see it now as through the eyes of a bird
A look that is fresh and new.

I begin to glide among the treetops
And see the beauty that Mother has created
It is here that I can unburden myself
Of all that is keeping my spirit deflated.

I drop over the side all that is keeping me down
The troubles and worries float away from my soul
I feel lighter and lighter as I rise up in the air
A feeling that brings comfort and tells me I am whole.

The air is clear and the world is fresh
A rebirth is beginning to take place
Higher and higher, lighter and lighter
I am surrounded by a heavenly grace.

As I leave the boundaries of the world below
The balloon unfurls and the colors come apart
They wrap themselves around me in a protective cloak
And begin to heal my body, my soul and my heart.

Higher and higher I still rise above
Until I see the Light that fills the space
The hands of the Spirit reach out to me
And I know I am in a special place.

My angel stands beside me,
And we are in a radiant glow
As my guides and family are smiling at me
Their strength and love begin to flow.

I feel them helping me to heal
They show that I have courage and that I am strong
I am blessed to be in their holy presence
And together we praise God in a soulful song.

I know that when it is time to cross over
I will be met by the spirits who care for me
But for now as the Light begins to fade
I glide down toward the earth feeling light and free.

My colorful and protective wrap
Floats to the waiting balloon
It once again becomes part of it
And we sail past the stars and the moon

I am energized with my healing spirit
And am ready to face my days
With the courage and love I found above
And I know my life is special in so many ways.

Once again I see the world from the atmosphere up high
And as the earthly beauty comes back into sight
I feel myself ready to take my place
Knowing that I have been blessed by God's holy Light.

As the balloon gently touches down
My cares and worries are not to be found
I have wisdom and courage, strength and love
I feel ready meet the world as my feet touch the ground.

I walk into this special place,
My home, my earth and my world
My angel is holding my hand
And together we are bold.

I am showered with grace
I am in the circle of light
I am loved and I love
Protected; My world is all right.

The Butterfly Is Me
Written February 23, 2003

Wrapped in the chrysalis safe and warm
There is a life being nurtured, about to transform.
Wintering away on the branch of a tree
A miracle of nature is waiting for me.

The eggs were laid and the caterpillar was born
She shed her skins in the warm autumn morn
And after a while when the time was just right
She cloaked herself in a pupa for the long winter's night.

The earth begins to warm and springtime arrive
With beauty and vibrancy, nature comes alive.
The butterfly emerges from its tight little world
To flutter and fly with her wings unfurled.

To be who she is has not been without pain
But to break out her safe world is how she can gain
Gain the freedom to live in the rain and the sun,
The freedom to be all that she will become.

Her colorful wings allow her to take flight
To taste the nectar of the flowers and bushes so bright
She is so delicate, but ever so strong
As she takes her place where she belongs.

The butterfly is a symbol for me
My totem, my strength; it allows me to be free
The struggles and hardships of finding myself
Help me, as the butterfly, to appreciate the wealth.

The wealth is the earth with its flowers and trees
The mountains and deserts, the sun and the breeze
The colors, the rivers, the lake and the stream
Are what I found when I awoke from the dream.

The real world presents many hardships and tears
But to be part of it diminishes the fears.
I try not to be afraid of what lies ahead
I live, not in the future, but in the present instead.

I spread my wings as my butterfly takes flight
I am finding my way through the day and night.
I live for the lessons that are here each day
And learn to love as I work and play.

To live in this world and be one with the Mother
Is to grow and to discover I am like no other
I, like my butterfly, am beautiful and free
And together we are part of all Eternity.

Miracles Abound
Written March 21, 2003

In my search for miracles and sacred places
I look to Nature and find all of the traces
Of spirit and soul in waterfalls and streams
The flowers and butterflies are part of these dreams.

I wander to sites where the beauty abounds
To special places where energy is found
Alaska, Hawaii, and the great Southwest
These are the places where I direct my quest.

I stand in awe of the majestic mountains
The canyons and temples and bubbling fountains.
My spirit fills with the power of the Divine
As I breathe in the scent of every flower and vine.

I need to see the sites that are amazingly grand
I feel I belong when I am in the Arizona sand.
When I look upon the colors and waves of the sea
I am part of them; and they, a part of me.

But the miracle of Creation is found everywhere
The rocks and the soil and the trees when they're bare
The bulbs that are sleeping through the long winter's night
And then awaken to the sun's brilliant light.

As springtime arrives with the warmth on the breeze
The flowers bloom and there are buds on the trees
The song of the birds fills the air with their tunes
And butterflies emerge from their tight cocoons.

Life is a miracle I experience each day
In the beauty of the sunrise and the birds at play.
As I dig in the ground to plant new seed
I feel the earth and my soul begins to feed.

I anxiously wait for the forsythia to flower
Sending out its blooms in a golden bower
As the gentle rain brings out the crocus
It is on the Creator that I find my focus.

The grass turns green and the birds are in flight
The daffodils and tulips color the world so bright
It is here in the rainbow of Nature's beauty
That the voice of God whispers to me.

On warm spring days my spirit is free
The smell, the sight and the sound nourish me.
The miracles are here each day in great number
In grandeur and simplicity; in wakefulness and slumber.

Rebirth and growing takes place in this season
And I am reminded that this life has a reason
I grow in this spiral of Creation on earth
I am connected to God and feel my worth.

Love on a Mountain Top
Written 2003

The spiral path leads me to the top of the mountain
Where I seek peace, joy and love.
My butterflies greet me as I reach the peak
And my spirit guides reach out their hands from the Goddess above.

The spiral continues in the labyrinth that my guides and I approach.
We are filled with the rhythms of the world
And holding hands, we dance the path,
Floating and moving with freedom, we bend and swirl.

The breath of our Mother is leading us on.
I feel her warmth as she kisses my cheek
My heart beats with her love that is filling my soul
And as we reach the center, the dance is complete.

I become rooted to the earth, as a tree strong and tall
I am One with the Goddess and I feel a great peace.
As I reach out to receive the blessings She brings,
I feel the love in me beginning to increase.

I stand with the Earth and great joy fills my soul
And a shower of rose petals rains down on me.
The colors are vivid and full of healing and love
I hold them close, smelling the fragrance that enhances their beauty.

I throw them into the air on a gentle wind
Sending out my love for others to receive
They are tossed about in a dance high in the air
And come together as a rainbow arcing over the trees.

The rainbow wraps itself around me
Bringing the energy of love and healing
The colors separate and go to the charkas
Leaving me with a Divine feeling.

My healing angel holds me in her loving arms
And we sway with the music that fills my soul
The colors flow back into the rainbow that is protecting me
Leaving me feeling safe and whole.

As we spiral back down from the mountain top
My butterfly sits upon my shoulder
A journey of love and joy has been taken
And my spirit is alive and a little bolder.

Love is the lesson I am learning today
The Goddess brings it to me
When I love myself I can give it to others
And then my spirit is alive and free.

Facts About Inflammatory Breast Cancer
From the National Cancer Institute
Fact Sheets

Key Points

- Inflammatory breast cancer is an uncommon type of breast cancer.

- This disease occurs when cancer cells block the lymph vessels in the skin of the breast, causing the breast to become red, swollen, and warm.

- Inflammatory breast cancer usually grows rapidly and often spreads to other parts of the body.

- Treatment usually starts with chemotherapy, generally followed by surgery and/or radiation.

Inflammatory breast cancer is an uncommon type of breast cancer in which breast cancer cells block the lymph vessels in the skin of the breast. This blockage may cause the breast to become red, swollen, and warm. The skin of the breast may also appear pink, purple, or bruised, and it may have ridges or appear pitted, like the skin of an orange (called peau d'orange). These changes often occur quickly over a period of weeks. Another possible sign of this type of breast cancer is swollen lymph nodes under the arm, above the collarbone, or in both places. Often, a tumor cannot be felt, and may not be seen on a mammogram. The diagnosis of inflammatory breast cancer is based on the results of the biopsy and the doctor's clinical judgment.

Inflammatory breast cancer generally grows rapidly, and the cancer cells often spread to other parts of the body. A woman with inflammatory breast cancer usually has local treatment to remove or destroy the cancer in the breast and systemic treatment to control or kill cancer cells that may have spread to other parts of the body. Local treatment affects only cells in the tumor and the area close to it; systemic treatment affects cells throughout the body. The local treatment may be surgery and/or radiation therapy to the breast and underarm. The systemic treatment may be chemotherapy (anticancer drugs), hormonal therapy (drugs that interfere with the effects of the female hormone estrogen), or both. Systemic treatment is generally given before surgery and/or radiation therapy. In some cases, local treatment may be followed by additional systemic treatment with hormonal therapy, chemotherapy, or both. Some women also may have biological therapy (which stimulates the immune system to fight the cancer).

Researchers continue to study the effectiveness of biological therapy, new chemotherapy and hormonal therapy, and new combinations of chemotherapy and hormonal therapy. Information about ongoing clinical trials (research studies) is available from the Cancer Information Service (see below), or from the clinical trials page of the National Cancer Institute's (NCI) Cancer.gov Web site at http://www.cancer.gov/clinical_trials on the Internet.

Facts About Inflammatory Breast Cancer
From the Inflammatory Breast Cancer
Research Center
www.ibcresearch.org

What is Inflammatory Breast Cancer?

INFLAMMATORY BREAST CANCER (IBC) is an advanced and accelerated form of breast cancer usually not detected by mammograms or ultrasounds. Inflammatory breast cancer requires immediate aggressive treatment with chemotherapy prior to surgery and is treated differently than more common types of breast cancer. African Americans have a higher incidence of IBC than do Caucasians and other ethnic groups (10.1%, 6.2%, and 5.1%, respectively).[1]

There is more than one kind of breast cancer.

We have been taught and are reminded frequently by public service announcements and by the medical community that when a woman discovers a lump on her breast she should go to the doctor immediately.

Inflammatory breast cancer usually grows in nests or sheets, rather than as a confined, solid tumor and therefore can be diffuse throughout the breast with no palpable mass. The cancer cells clog the lymphatic system just below the skin. Lymph node involvement is assumed. Increased breast density compared to prior mammograms should be considered suspicious.

You Don't Have to Have a Lump to Have Breast Cancer

Some women who have inflammatory breast cancer may remain undiagnosed for long periods, even while seeing their doctor to learn the cause of her symptoms. The symptoms are similar to

---

1. Cristofanilli M, Buzdar AU, Hortobágyi G. Update on the Management of Inflammatory Breast Cancer. The Oncologist 2003;8:141-148.

mastitis, a breast infection and some doctors, not recognizing IBC, will prescribe antibiotics. If a response to antibiotics is not apparent after a week, a biopsy should be performed or a referral to a breast specialist is warranted.

Age 52: Median age at time of diagnosis of IBC...

A surprising portion of young women with IBC had their first symptoms during pregnancy or lactation. The misconception that these young women are at lower risk for breast cancer and the fact that IBC is the most aggressive form of breast cancer may result in metastases when the diagnosis is made.

...versus, Age 62: Median age at time of diagnosis of Breast Cancer

One or more of the following are Typical Symptoms of IBC:

- Swelling, usually sudden, sometimes a cup size in a few days
- Itching
- Pink, red, or dark colored area (called erythema) sometimes with texture similar to the skin of an orange (called peau d'orange)
- Ridges and thickened areas of the skin
- What appears to be a bruise that does not go away
- Nipple retraction
- Nipple discharge, may or may not be bloody
- Breast is warm to the touch
- Breast pain (from a constant ache to stabbing pains)
- Change in color and texture of the aureole

These Symptoms May Be Present in Benign Breast Disorders See your doctor if you have any of these symptoms.

Inflammatory Breast Cancer is typically abbreviated as IBC. Non-inflammatory breast cancer may include in its diagnosis the terms "in situ breast cancer," "infiltrating breast cancer," or "invasive breast cancer" all of which may be abbreviated with "ibc," but those terms alone do not specify inflammatory breast cancer. To add to the possible confusion, the diagnosis may include more that one kind of breast cancer; for example "inflammatory breast cancer, invasive ductal carcinoma, and mucinous carcinoma" all in the same breast. So if a person you know has been described as having ibc, it may be well to ask what that is abbreviating, since it may not be "inflammatory breast cancer" and therefore the symptoms and other information presented here may not apply.

Disclaimer

This book designed for educational and inspirational purposes only and is not engaged in rendering medical advice. The information provided through this book should not be used for diagnosing or treating a health problem or a disease. It is not a substitute for professional care.

If you have a health problem or suspect that you may have a health problem, you should consult your health care provider.

The authors, editors, producers, sponsors, and contributors shall have no liability, obligation or responsibility to any person or entity for any loss, damage, or adverse consequence alleged to have happened directly or indirectly as a consequence of any material provided in this book.

Printed in the United States
67563LVS00005B/592-612